GRATITUDE DIARY

A GIFT FOR YOU

This Diary belongs to

_____

Copyright © 2022 Brenda Nathan

All rights reserved.

ISBN: 978-1-952358-33-3

Gratitude

Gratitude is a feeling of appreciation for what one has. It is a feeling of thankfulness for the blessings we have received. Cultivating an attitude of gratitude yields many benefits: physical, mental and spiritual. Feeling gratitude in the present moment makes you happier and more relaxed, and improves your overall health and well-being.

Gratitude doesn't just have to be about the big things. It can also be for small, everyday events. You can be thankful for simple things such as enjoying a movie or just talking to an old friend for the first time in a long while. There is always something that you can be grateful for in your life. It is all about appreciating the things around you rather than taking them all for granted.

There is an exercise at the beginning of this diary to complete before starting your daily record of gratitude. It will help get you familiar with feeling gratitude and appreciation. There are also pages where you can just draw something. If you don't feel like drawing anything, simply paste a beautiful picture onto this page.

Gratitude makes us more optimistic and compassionate. By keeping a record of your gratitude in a diary, you will store positive energy, gain clarity in your life, and have greater control of your thoughts and emotions.

Each day, write down three to five things that you are grateful for in this diary and turn your ordinary moments into blessings.

People I am *Grateful* for:

Top 10 things that I was scared to do but am now *Grateful* for having done:

1.
2.
3.
4.
5.
6.
7.
8.
9.
10.

People I have made a difference to and am *Grateful* for having had this opportunity:

Top 10 places I have visited and am *Grateful* for:

1.
2.
3.
4.
5.
6.
7.
8.
9.
10.

The times when I have laughed so hard
that I cried and which I am now *Grateful* for:

Top 10 memorable events in my life that
I am *Grateful* for:

1.
2.
3.
4.
5.
6.
7.
8.
9.
10.

Day: _____ *Date:* _____

Today I am *Grateful* for _____

_____

_____

_____

_____

The art of being happy lies in the power of extracting happiness from common things. ~ *Henry Ward Beecher*

Day: _____ *Date:* _____

Today I am *Grateful* for _____

_____

_____

_____

_____

Day: _____ *Date:* ____ / ____ / ____

Today I am *Grateful* for _____

_____

_____

_____

_____

_____

_____

Happiness is not an ideal of reason, but of imagination. ~ *Immanuel Kant*

Day: _____ *Date:* ____ / ____ / ____

Today I am *Grateful* for _____

_____

_____

_____

_____

_____

_____

Day: _____ *Date:* ____/____/____

Today I am *Grateful* for _____

_____
_____
_____
_____
_____

The essence of all beautiful art, all great art, is gratitude. ~ *Friedrich Nietzsche*

Day: _____ *Date:* ____/____/____

Today I am *Grateful* for _____

_____
_____
_____
_____
_____

Day: _____ *Date:* ____/____/____

Today I am *Grateful* for _____

_____
_____
_____
_____
_____

> There is only one way to happiness and that is to cease worrying about things which are beyond the power of our will. ~ *Epictetus*

Day: _____ *Date:* ____/____/____

Today I am *Grateful* for _____

_____
_____
_____
_____
_____

Day: _____ *Date:* _____

Today I am *Grateful* for _____

_____

_____

_____

_____

_____

_____

Our greatest glory is not in never falling, but in rising every time we fall.
~ *Confucius*

Day: _____ *Date:* _____

Today I am *Grateful* for _____

_____

_____

_____

_____

_____

_____

Day: _____ *Date:* ____/____/____

Today I am *Grateful* for _____

_____
_____
_____
_____
_____
_____

> Positive anything is better than negative nothing.
> ~ *Elbert Hubbard*

Day: _____ *Date:* ____/____/____

Today I am *Grateful* for _____

_____
_____
_____
_____
_____
_____

Day: _____ *Date:* ___/___/___

Today I am *Grateful* for _____

_____
_____
_____
_____
_____

> The direction of the mind is more important than its progress.
> ~ Joseph Joubert

Day: _____ *Date:* ___/___/___

Today I am *Grateful* for _____

_____
_____
_____
_____
_____

Day: _____ *Date:* ____ / ____ / ____

Today I am *Grateful* for _____

_____

_____

_____

_____

_____

> If the only prayer you say in your life is thank you, that would suffice.
> ~ *Meister Eckhart*

Day: _____ *Date:* ____ / ____ / ____

Today I am *Grateful* for _____

_____

_____

_____

_____

_____

Day: _____ *Date:* ____/____/____

Today I am *Grateful* for _____

_____

_____

_____

_____

_____

Courtesies of a small and trivial character are the ones which strike deepest in the grateful and appreciating heart. ~ *Henry Clay*

Day: _____ *Date:* ____/____/____

Today I am *Grateful* for _____

_____

_____

_____

_____

_____

Day: _____ *Date:* _____/_____/_____

Today I am *Grateful* for _____

_____
_____
_____
_____
_____
_____

Gratitude is a state of being and should be directed towards everything that you are creating in this life.

Day: _____ *Date:* _____/_____/_____

Today I am *Grateful* for _____

_____
_____
_____
_____
_____
_____

Day: _____ *Date:* ___/___/___

Today I am *Grateful* for _____

_____

_____

_____

_____

Happiness resides not in possessions, and not in gold, happiness dwells in the soul. ~ *Democritus*

Day: _____ *Date:* ___/___/___

Today I am *Grateful* for _____

_____

_____

_____

_____

Day: _____ *Date:* ____/____/____

Today I am *Grateful* for _____

_____
_____
_____
_____
_____

A daily practice of appreciation can transform one's life.

Day: _____ *Date:* ____/____/____

Today I am *Grateful* for _____

_____
_____
_____
_____
_____

Day: Date: /   /

Today I am *Grateful* for

Things do not change; we change. ~ *Henry David Thoreau*

Day: Date: /   /

Today I am *Grateful* for

Day: _____ *Date:* ____ / ____ / ____

Today I am *Grateful* for _____

_____
_____
_____
_____
_____
_____
_____

The clearest way into the Universe is through a forest wilderness. ~ *John Muir*

Day: _____ *Date:* ____ / ____ / ____

Today I am *Grateful* for _____

_____
_____
_____
_____
_____
_____
_____

Draw something

Day: _____ *Date:* ____/____/____

Today I am *Grateful* for _____

_____

_____

_____

_____

_____

Gratitude is the sign of noble souls. ~ *Aesop Fables*

Day: _____ *Date:* ____/____/____

Today I am *Grateful* for _____

_____

_____

_____

_____

_____

Day: _____ *Date:* ___/___/___

Today I am *Grateful* for _____

_____

_____

_____

_____

Gratitude is not only the greatest of virtues, but the parent of all the others.
~ *Marcus Tullius Cicero*

Day: _____ *Date:* ___/___/___

Today I am *Grateful* for _____

_____

_____

_____

_____

Day: _____ *Date:* ____ / ____ / ____

Today I am *Grateful* for _____

_____
_____
_____
_____
_____

> The pleasure which we most rarely experience gives us greatest delight.
> ~ *Epictetus*

Day: _____ *Date:* ____ / ____ / ____

Today I am *Grateful* for _____

_____
_____
_____
_____
_____

Day: _____ Date: ____/____/____

Today I am *Grateful* for _____

_____
_____
_____
_____
_____

Showing up is the most important thing you can do for a friend.

Day: _____ Date: ____/____/____

Today I am *Grateful* for _____

_____
_____
_____
_____
_____

Day: _____ *Date:* ____/____/____

Today I am *Grateful* for

If a little dreaming is dangerous, the cure for it is not to dream less but to dream more, to dream all the time. ~ *Marcel Proust*

Day: _____ *Date:* ____/____/____

Today I am *Grateful* for

Day: _____ *Date:* ____/____/____

Today I am *Grateful* for _____

_____
_____
_____
_____
_____

> Gratitude is a duty which ought to be paid, but which none have a right to expect. ~ *Jean-Jacques Rousseau*

Day: _____ *Date:* ____/____/____

Today I am *Grateful* for _____

_____
_____
_____
_____
_____

Day: _____ *Date:* ____ / ____ / ____

Today I am *Grateful* for _____

_____

_____

_____

_____

_____

_____

Appreciation is a wonderful thing: It makes what is excellent in others belong to us as well. ~ *Voltaire*

Day: _____ *Date:* ____ / ____ / ____

Today I am *Grateful* for _____

_____

_____

_____

_____

_____

_____

Day: _____ *Date:* ___/___/___

Today I am *Grateful* for

_____
_____
_____
_____
_____
_____

> Believe you can and you're halfway there.
> ~ *Theodore Roosevelt*

Day: _____ *Date:* ___/___/___

Today I am *Grateful* for

_____
_____
_____
_____
_____
_____

Day: _____ *Date:* ____ / ____ / ____

Today I am *Grateful* for _____

_____
_____
_____
_____
_____

When unhappy, one doubts everything; when happy, one doubts nothing.
~ *Joseph Roux*

Day: _____ *Date:* ____ / ____ / ____

Today I am *Grateful* for _____

_____
_____
_____
_____
_____

Day: _____ *Date:* ___/___/___

Today I am *Grateful* for _____

_____

_____

_____

_____

Our happiness depends on wisdom all the way. ~ *Sophocles*

Day: _____ *Date:* ___/___/___

Today I am *Grateful* for _____

_____

_____

_____

_____

Day: _____ *Date:* ____/____/____

Today I am *Grateful* for _____

_____
_____
_____
_____
_____
_____

The most certain sign of wisdom is cheerfulness. ~ *Michel de Montaigne*

Day: _____ *Date:* ____/____/____

Today I am *Grateful* for _____

_____
_____
_____
_____
_____
_____

Day: *Date:*

Today I am *Grateful* for

> To live is so startling it leaves little time for anything else.
> ~ *Emily Dickinson*

Day: *Date:*

Today I am *Grateful* for

Day: _____ *Date:* ___/___/___

Today I am *Grateful* for _____

_____

_____

_____

_____

_____

> A single grateful thought toward heaven is the most perfect prayer.
> ~ *Gotthold Ephraim Lessing*

Day: _____ *Date:* ___/___/___

Today I am *Grateful* for _____

_____

_____

_____

_____

_____

Day: Date:

Today I am *Grateful* for

Everything has beauty, but not everyone sees it. ~ *Confucius*

Day: Date:

Today I am *Grateful* for

Draw something

Day: *Date:*

Today I am *Grateful* for

Surround yourself with positive people who can raise you to a higher level.

Day: *Date:*

Today I am *Grateful* for

Day: _____ *Date:* ____ / ____ / ____

Today I am *Grateful* for _____

_____
_____
_____
_____
_____
_____

Let us learn to appreciate there will be times when the trees will be bare, and look forward to the time when we may pick the fruit. ~ *Anton Chekhov*

Day: _____ *Date:* ____ / ____ / ____

Today I am *Grateful* for _____

_____
_____
_____
_____
_____
_____

Day: _____ *Date:* ___/___/___

Today I am *Grateful* for _____

_____

_____

_____

_____

A contented mind is the greatest blessing a man can enjoy in this world.
~ *Joseph Addison*

Day: _____ *Date:* ___/___/___

Today I am *Grateful* for _____

_____

_____

_____

_____

Day: _____ *Date:* ____/____/____

Today I am *Grateful* for

Good actions give strength to ourselves and inspire good actions in others.
~ *Plato*

Day: _____ *Date:* ____/____/____

Today I am *Grateful* for

Day: _____ *Date:* ___/___/___

Today I am *Grateful* for _____

_____

_____

_____

_____

Our best successes often come after our greatest disappointments.
~ *Henry Ward Beecher*

Day: _____ *Date:* ___/___/___

Today I am *Grateful* for _____

_____

_____

_____

_____

Day: _____ *Date:* ____/____/____

Today I am *Grateful* for _____

_____
_____
_____
_____
_____

A loving heart is the beginning of all knowledge. ~ *Thomas Carlyle*

Day: _____ *Date:* ____/____/____

Today I am *Grateful* for _____

_____
_____
_____
_____
_____

Day: _____ *Date:* ___/___/___

Today I am *Grateful* for _____

_____

_____

_____

_____

_____

Honesty is the first chapter in the book of wisdom. ~ *Thomas Jefferson*

Day: _____ *Date:* ___/___/___

Today I am *Grateful* for _____

_____

_____

_____

_____

_____

Day: _____ Date: ____/____/____

Today I am *Grateful* for _____

_____
_____
_____
_____
_____
_____

Life in abundance comes only through great love.
~ *Elbert Hubbard*

Day: _____ Date: ____/____/____

Today I am *Grateful* for _____

_____
_____
_____
_____
_____
_____

Day: _____ *Date:* ___/___/___

Today I am *Grateful* for _____

_____
_____
_____
_____

The mountains are calling and I must go. ~ *John Muir*

Day: _____ *Date:* ___/___/___

Today I am *Grateful* for _____

_____
_____
_____
_____

Day: _____ *Date:* ____/____/____

Today I am *Grateful* for _____

_____
_____
_____
_____
_____

The way to know life is to love many things. ~ *Vincent Van Gogh*

Day: _____ *Date:* ____/____/____

Today I am *Grateful* for _____

_____
_____
_____
_____
_____

Day: _____ *Date:* ____/____/____

Today I am *Grateful* for _____

_____

_____

_____

_____

It takes less time to do a thing right, than it does to explain why you did it wrong. ~ *Henry Wadsworth Longfellow*

Day: _____ *Date:* ____/____/____

Today I am *Grateful* for _____

_____

_____

_____

_____

Day: _____ *Date:* ____/____/____

Today I am *Grateful* for _____

_____
_____
_____
_____
_____

> Keep love in your heart. A life without it is like a sunless garden when the flowers are dead. ~ *Oscar Wilde*

Day: _____ *Date:* ____/____/____

Today I am *Grateful* for _____

_____
_____
_____
_____
_____

Day: _____ *Date:* ____/____/____

Today I am *Grateful* for

_____
_____
_____
_____
_____

By doubting we are led to question, by questioning we arrive at the truth.
~ *Peter Abelard*

Day: _____ *Date:* ____/____/____

Today I am *Grateful* for

_____
_____
_____
_____
_____

Day: _____ *Date:* ____ / ____ / ____

Today I am *Grateful* for _____

_____
_____
_____
_____
_____
_____

Never do a wrong thing to make a friend or to keep one. ~ *Robert E. Lee*

Day: _____ *Date:* ____ / ____ / ____

Today I am *Grateful* for _____

_____
_____
_____
_____
_____
_____

Draw something

Day: _____ *Date:* ____/____/____

Today I am *Grateful* for _____

_____

_____

_____

_____

_____

_____

Life consists not in holding good cards but in playing those you hold well.
~ *Josh Billings*

Day: _____ *Date:* ____/____/____

Today I am *Grateful* for _____

_____

_____

_____

_____

_____

_____

Day: _____ *Date:* ____/____/____

Today I am *Grateful* for

_____
_____
_____
_____
_____
_____

Nothing is a waste of time if you use the experience wisely. ~ *Auguste Rodin*

Day: _____ *Date:* ____/____/____

Today I am *Grateful* for

_____
_____
_____
_____
_____
_____

Day: _____ *Date:* _____ / _____ / _____

Today I am *Grateful* for _____

_____

_____

_____

_____

_____

_____

He who knows best knows how little he knows. ~ *Thomas Jefferson*

Day: _____ *Date:* _____ / _____ / _____

Today I am *Grateful* for _____

_____

_____

_____

_____

_____

_____

Day: _____ *Date:* ___/___/___

Today I am *Grateful* for _____

_____

_____

_____

_____

_____

Great thoughts speak only to the thoughtful mind, but great actions speak to all mankind. ~ *Theodore Roosevelt*

Day: _____ *Date:* ___/___/___

Today I am *Grateful* for _____

_____

_____

_____

_____

_____

Day: _____ *Date:* ____/____/____

Today I am *Grateful* for _____

_____

_____

_____

_____

_____

_____

Never give up, for that is just the place and time that the tide will turn.
~ *Harriet Beecher Stowe*

Day: _____ *Date:* ____/____/____

Today I am *Grateful* for _____

_____

_____

_____

_____

_____

_____

Day: _____ *Date:* ____/____/____

Today I am *Grateful* for
_____
_____
_____
_____
_____

Either I will find a way, or I will make one. ~ *Philip Sidney*

Day: _____ *Date:* ____/____/____

Today I am *Grateful* for
_____
_____
_____
_____
_____

Day: _____ *Date:* ____/____/____

Today I am *Grateful* for _____

_____

_____

_____

_____

_____

Do not fear mistakes. You will know failure. Continue to reach out.
~ *Benjamin Franklin*

Day: _____ *Date:* ____/____/____

Today I am *Grateful* for _____

_____

_____

_____

_____

_____

Day: _____ *Date:* ____/____/____

Today I am *Grateful* for _____

_____
_____
_____
_____
_____
_____

It is costly wisdom that is bought by experience. ~ *Roger Ascham*

Day: _____ *Date:* ____/____/____

Today I am *Grateful* for _____

_____
_____
_____
_____
_____
_____

Day: _____ Date: ____/____/____

Today I am *Grateful* for _____

_____

_____

_____

_____

_____

To love oneself is the beginning of a lifelong romance. ~ *Oscar Wilde*

Day: _____ Date: ____/____/____

Today I am *Grateful* for _____

_____

_____

_____

_____

_____

Day: _____ Date: ___/___/___

Today I am *Grateful* for _____

_____
_____
_____
_____

We have it in our power to begin the world over again. ~ *Thomas Paine*

Day: _____ Date: ___/___/___

Today I am *Grateful* for _____

_____
_____
_____
_____

Day: _____ *Date:* ____/____/____

Today I am *Grateful* for _____

_____
_____
_____
_____
_____

Habit, if not resisted, soon becomes necessity. ~ *Saint Augustine*

Day: _____ *Date:* ____/____/____

Today I am *Grateful* for _____

_____
_____
_____
_____
_____

Day: _____ *Date:* ___/___/___

Today I am *Grateful* for

_____
_____
_____
_____
_____

Ask me not what I have, but what I am. ~ *Heinrich Heine*

Day: _____ *Date:* ___/___/___

Today I am *Grateful* for

_____
_____
_____
_____
_____

Day: _____ *Date:* ____ / ____ / ____

Today I am *Grateful* for

The best preparation for tomorrow is to do today's work superbly well.
~ William Osler

Day: _____ *Date:* ____ / ____ / ____

Today I am *Grateful* for

Day: Date: /   /

Today I am *Grateful* for

Where there is unity there is always victory. ~ *Publilius Syrus*

Day: Date: /   /

Today I am *Grateful* for

Draw something

Day: _____ Date: _____

Today I am *Grateful* for

What you think you are, you are, until you think otherwise.
~ *American Proverb*

Day: _____ Date: ___/___/___

Today I am *Grateful* for

Day: _____ *Date:* ____ / ____ / ____

Today I am *Grateful* for

> Little minds are interested in the extraordinary; great minds in the commonplace. ~ *Elbert Hubbard*

Day: _____ *Date:* ____ / ____ / ____

Today I am *Grateful* for

Day: _____ *Date:* _____

Today I am *Grateful* for

Do not mind anything that anyone tells you about anyone else.
Judge everyone and everything for yourself. ~ *Henry James*

Day: _____ *Date:* _____

Today I am *Grateful* for

Day: _____ *Date:* ____ / ____ / ____

Today I am *Grateful* for _____

_____
_____
_____
_____
_____

It is our attitude at the beginning of a difficult task which, more than anything else, will affect its successful outcome. ~ *William James*

Day: _____ *Date:* ____ / ____ / ____

Today I am *Grateful* for _____

_____
_____
_____
_____
_____

Day: *Date:*

Today I am *Grateful* for

Cheerfulness is the best promoter of health and is as friendly to the mind as to the body. ~ *Joseph Addison*

Day: *Date:*

Today I am *Grateful* for

Day: _____ *Date:* ____/____/____

Today I am *Grateful* for _____

_____
_____
_____
_____
_____

Do whatever you do intensely. ~ *Robert Henri*

Day: _____ *Date:* ____/____/____

Today I am *Grateful* for _____

_____
_____
_____
_____
_____

Day: _____ *Date:* ____/____/____

Today I am *Grateful* for

_____

_____

_____

_____

_____

_____

It is never too late to be what you might have been. ~ *George Eliot*

Day: _____ *Date:* ____/____/____

Today I am *Grateful* for

_____

_____

_____

_____

_____

_____

Day: _____ *Date:* ___/___/___

Today I am *Grateful* for _____

_____
_____
_____
_____
_____

> A thing of beauty is a joy forever: its loveliness increases; it will never pass into nothingness. ~ *John Keats*

Day: _____ *Date:* ___/___/___

Today I am *Grateful* for _____

_____
_____
_____
_____
_____

Day: _____ *Date:* ____/____/____

Today I am *Grateful* for _____

_____
_____
_____
_____

> To have courage for whatever comes in life - everything lies in that.
> *~ Saint Teresa of Avila*

Day: _____ *Date:* ____/____/____

Today I am *Grateful* for _____

_____
_____
_____
_____

Day: _____ *Date:* ____ / ____ / ____

Today I am *Grateful* for _____

_____

_____

_____

_____

_____

We build too many walls and not enough bridges. ~ *Isaac Newton*

Day: _____ *Date:* ____ / ____ / ____

Today I am *Grateful* for _____

_____

_____

_____

_____

_____

Day:　　　　　　　*Date:*

Today I am *Grateful* for

After a storm comes a calm. ~ *Matthew Henry*

Day:　　　　　　　*Date:*

Today I am *Grateful* for

Day: _____ *Date:* ____ / ____ / ____

Today I am *Grateful* for _____

_____

_____

_____

_____

_____

> A thousand words will not leave so deep an impression as one deed.
> ~ *Henrik Ibsen*

Day: _____ *Date:* ____ / ____ / ____

Today I am *Grateful* for _____

_____

_____

_____

_____

_____

Day: _____ *Date:* ____/____/____

Today I am *Grateful* for _____

_____
_____
_____
_____

All experience is an arch, to build upon. ~ *Henry Adams*

Day: _____ *Date:* ____/____/____

Today I am *Grateful* for _____

_____
_____
_____
_____

Day: _____ *Date:* ____/____/____

Today I am *Grateful* for _____

_____
_____
_____
_____
_____

Thank God every morning when you get up that you have something to do that day, which must be done, whether you like it or not. ~ *James Russell Lowell*

Day: _____ *Date:* ____/____/____

Today I am *Grateful* for _____

_____
_____
_____
_____
_____

Draw something

Day: _____ *Date:* ____ / ____ / ____

Today I am *Grateful* for _____

_____

_____

_____

_____

_____

> Genius is the ability to renew one's emotions in daily experience.
> ~ *Paul Cezanne*

Day: _____ *Date:* ____ / ____ / ____

Today I am *Grateful* for _____

_____

_____

_____

_____

_____

Day: _____ *Date:* ___/___/___

Today I am *Grateful* for _____

_____

_____

_____

_____

_____

How very little can be done under the spirit of fear. ~ *Florence Nightingale*

Day: _____ *Date:* ___/___/___

Today I am *Grateful* for _____

_____

_____

_____

_____

_____

Day: _____ *Date:* ____/____/____

Today I am *Grateful* for _____

_____
_____
_____
_____

> Doubt comes in at the window when inquiry is denied at the door.
> ~ *Benjamin Jowett*

Day: _____ *Date:* ____/____/____

Today I am *Grateful* for _____

_____
_____
_____
_____

Day: _____   *Date:* ___/___/___

Today I am *Grateful* for

_____
_____
_____
_____
_____
_____

Life is not a matter of holding good cards, but of playing a poor hand well.
~ *Robert Louis Stevenson*

Day: _____   *Date:* ___/___/___

Today I am *Grateful* for

_____
_____
_____
_____
_____
_____

Day: _____ *Date:* ____/____/____

Today I am *Grateful* for _____

_____
_____
_____
_____
_____
_____

> With an eye made quiet by the power of harmony, and the deep power of joy, we see into the life of things. ~ *William Wordsworth*

Day: _____ *Date:* ____/____/____

Today I am *Grateful* for _____

_____
_____
_____
_____
_____
_____

Day: _____   *Date:* ____/____/____

Today I am *Grateful* for _____

_____
_____
_____
_____
_____

We consume our tomorrows fretting about our yesterdays. ~ *Persius*

Day: _____   *Date:* ____/____/____

Today I am *Grateful* for _____

_____
_____
_____
_____
_____

Day: _____ *Date:* _____ / _____ / _____

Today I am *Grateful* for _____

_____

_____

_____

_____

_____

A gentle word, a kind look, a good-natured smile can work wonders and accomplish miracles. ~ *William Hazlitt*

Day: _____ *Date:* _____ / _____ / _____

Today I am *Grateful* for _____

_____

_____

_____

_____

_____

Day: _____   Date: ___/___/___

Today I am *Grateful* for _____

_____
_____
_____
_____
_____

No man is an island, entire of itself; every man is a piece of the continent.
~ *John Donne*

Day: _____   Date: ___/___/___

Today I am *Grateful* for _____

_____
_____
_____
_____
_____

Day: _____ *Date:* ____ / ____ / ____

Today I am *Grateful* for _____

_____
_____
_____
_____
_____

Live your life as though your every act were to become a universal law.
~ *Immanuel Kant*

Day: _____ *Date:* ____ / ____ / ____

Today I am *Grateful* for _____

_____
_____
_____
_____
_____

Day: *Date:*

Today I am *Grateful* for

If you want the present to be different from the past, study the past.
~ *Baruch Spinoza*

Day: *Date:*

Today I am *Grateful* for

Day: _____ *Date:* ____/____/____

Today I am *Grateful* for _____

_____
_____
_____
_____
_____
_____

> The measure of a man's real character is what he would do if he knew he would never be found out. ~ *Thomas Babington Macaulay*

Day: _____ *Date:* ____/____/____

Today I am *Grateful* for _____

_____
_____
_____
_____
_____
_____

Day: *Date:*

Today I am *Grateful* for

To be yourself in a world that is constantly trying to make you something else is the greatest achievement. ~ *Ralph Waldo Emerson*

Day: *Date:*

Today I am *Grateful* for

Day: _____ *Date:* ____ / ____ / ____

Today I am *Grateful* for _____

_____
_____
_____
_____
_____

Begin, be bold and venture to be wise. ~ *Horace*

Day: _____ *Date:* ____ / ____ / ____

Today I am *Grateful* for _____

_____
_____
_____
_____
_____

Day: Date: /   /

Today I am *Grateful* for

Of the blessings set before you make your choice, and be content.
~ Samuel Johnson

Day: Date: /   /

Today I am *Grateful* for

Draw something

Day: _____ *Date:* ___/___/___

Today I am *Grateful* for _____

I dwell in possibility. ~ *Emily Dickinson*

Day: _____ *Date:* ___/___/___

Today I am *Grateful* for _____

Day: _____ *Date:* ____/____/____

Today I am *Grateful* for

Let us be of good cheer, however, remembering that the misfortunes hardest to bear are those which never come. ~ *James Russell Lowell*

Day: _____ *Date:* ____/____/____

Today I am *Grateful* for

Day:					Date:		/	/

Today I am *Grateful* for

He who knows that enough is enough will always have enough.
~ Lao Tzu

Day:					Date:		/	/

Today I am *Grateful* for

Day: _____ *Date:* ____/____/____

Today I am *Grateful* for _____

_____

_____

_____

_____

_____

> You cannot do a kindness too soon, for you never know how soon it will be too late. ~ *Ralph Waldo Emerson*

Day: _____ *Date:* ____/____/____

Today I am *Grateful* for _____

_____

_____

_____

_____

_____

Day: Date:

Today I am *Grateful* for

_____

_____

_____

_____

_____

_____

Real happiness is cheap enough, yet how dearly we pay for its counterfeit.
~ *Hosea Ballou*

Day: Date:

Today I am *Grateful* for

_____

_____

_____

_____

_____

_____

Day: _____ *Date:* ____ / ____ / ____

Today I am *Grateful* for _____

_____
_____
_____
_____
_____
_____

He who would learn to fly one day must first learn to stand and walk and run and climb and dance; one cannot fly into flying. ~ *Friedrich Nietzsche*

Day: _____ *Date:* ____ / ____ / ____

Today I am *Grateful* for _____

_____
_____
_____
_____
_____
_____

Day: _____ *Date:* ___/___/___

Today I am *Grateful* for _____

_____

_____

_____

_____

_____

_____

The power of imagination makes us infinite. ~ *John Muir*

Day: _____ *Date:* ___/___/___

Today I am *Grateful* for _____

_____

_____

_____

_____

_____

_____

Day: _____ *Date:* ___/___/___

Today I am *Grateful* for _____

_____
_____
_____
_____
_____

Happiness is a choice that requires effort at times. ~ *Aeschylus*

Day: _____ *Date:* ___/___/___

Today I am *Grateful* for _____

_____
_____
_____
_____
_____

Day: _____ *Date:* _____

Today I am *Grateful* for

> What we obtain too cheap, we esteem too lightly; it is dearness only that gives everything its value. ~ *Thomas Paine*

Day: _____ *Date:* _____

Today I am *Grateful* for

Day: _____ *Date:* _____ / _____ / _____

Today I am *Grateful* for _____

_____

_____

_____

_____

_____

What worries you, masters you. ~ John Locke

Day: _____ *Date:* _____ / _____ / _____

Today I am *Grateful* for _____

_____

_____

_____

_____

_____

Day: *Date:*

Today I am *Grateful* for

All things are difficult before they are easy. ~ *Thomas Fuller*

Day: *Date:*

Today I am *Grateful* for

Day: _____ *Date:* ____/____/____

Today I am *Grateful* for _____

_____

_____

_____

_____

_____

Knowing is not enough; we must apply. Willing is not enough; we must do.
~ *Johann Wolfgang von Goethe*

Day: _____ *Date:* ____/____/____

Today I am *Grateful* for _____

_____

_____

_____

_____

_____

Day: *Date:* / /

Today I am *Grateful* for

The purpose creates the machine. ~ Arthur Young

Day: *Date:* / /

Today I am *Grateful* for

Day: _____ *Date:* ____/____/____

Today I am *Grateful* for _____

_____
_____
_____
_____
_____
_____

The trees that are slow to grow bear the best fruit. ~ *Moliere*

Day: _____ *Date:* ____/____/____

Today I am *Grateful* for _____

_____
_____
_____
_____
_____
_____

Draw something

Notes